In a Sense

By

Paul Girvan

impspired@gmail.com

Cover designed by Paul Girvan
Artwork by Paul Girvan

ISBN: 978-1-915819-75-8

To Sir Michael Nicholson
friend and colleague
who found my Muse

OTHER TITLES BY IMPSPIRED

Maybury –
by Mary Farrell

The Metaphysics of Now -
by Jim Bates

Menopausal Mermaids & Life Lines –
by Sinead Coxhill

Fetch -
by Yvonne Hamilton

Spun Tales and Woven Words –
by North Coast Writers

Cracking the Air –
by Jimmy Milliken

Fractured Echoes –
by Gerladine Fleming

IMPSPIRED

INTRODUCTION

One day out of the blue my judicial colleague and old friend, the late, Sir Michael Nicholson sent me and my judicial colleagues an e-mail containing the last line of a poem. He invited his colleagues to compose a poem to end in that last line. A creative writers' facilitator would doubtless call this a stimulus exercise, something to spark creative writing by the person challenged to write in response to the stimulus. For judges who spent most of their time using careful and unemotional words and language to analyse, explain and decide cases an invitation to write a poem was indeed something of a challenge. Among my judicial colleagues I alone decided to rise to the occasion. Thereafter for a time Michael would send out last lines with a similar invitation. I greatly enjoyed the experience of writing a poetic response to the challenges and thereafter I moved on to incorporating in poems ideas and themes that we judges discussed during lunchtime court recesses.

Mary Farrell to whom I refer more fully in the acknowledgments has encouraged me to add this collection of poems to the burgeoning North Coast Writers' library. I do so with some trepidation remembering the words of Thomas Kinsella: Ireland has many poets and most of them are no good.

The poems in this collection are divided into different thematic groupings. The first group are under the heading A Sense of Time and Place in which I explore the pervasive senses of time and place which can be evoked by what the ancient Romans called the genius loci. In the second group A Sense of Humour I seek to explore different more light-hearted experiences or themes. Poetry does not always need to be heavily emotional and serious after all. Many of the poems were stimulated by chats or discussions at judges' lunches. In A Sense of Judgment a light hearted approach to the judicial life prevails – judges are human beings after all! In a Sense of Tragedy I explore some of the darker realities of life. In a Sense of Occasion inter alia I recall a couple of great and colourful occasions which I attended in Dublin and which were designed to encourage greater rapport between the judges north and south. Following a brief experiment with romantic poetry I conclude with A Sense of an Ending the last poem of which takes me back to the beginning of my poetic odyssey. It was the poem I wrote in response to Michael Nicholson's last line challenge.

Foreword by Sue Steging recipient of the Seamus Heaney Award for New Writing 2023

From the first page of this, Paul's first collection, we sense that we are about to encounter a writer of great erudition. Reading these poems we discover the scope of Paul's knowledge and interests and share his enjoyment of language, rhythm, and rhyme – especially rhyme! We'll find that he isn't afraid to use archaic vocabulary, syntax, and metre where this will speed the music of the lines, calling to mind as he does so the links between past and present in the themes and scenes he shares with us. Paul is also a visual artist and it is perhaps not surprising then that he is quick to spot an opportunity for a concrete poem where the form will underscore its meaning, whether this exposes the sybaritic foundations of a 'temple' now serving as a viewpoint for an awe-inspiring view of the north Atlantic or the mirroring of the Venetian past in the waters of the Grand Canal.

Buildings also serve to concretise some of humanity's moral dilemmas. Judicial observations of dissipation and decadence sharpen his perception; he lifts the curtain on dramas that took place in buildings where themes of aspiration and ambivalence have been, and perhaps still are, enacted. Here he ranges widely from basilica and cathedral to the humble turf stack, casually introducing us to his fluency in French, Italian, Spanish and Irish as he goes.

Perhaps it is his facility with language that enables him to draw us along as he goes, exploring beneath the surface of cultures we might be happy to see only from the perspective of their shiny, often marbled, surfaces. Instead, we are gently directed to the comparisons to be made between now and then, here and there; sometimes allusive as when Irish and classical myth are brought to mind, sometimes more directly in the Disneyfication of San Gimignano or when we are asked to remember and mourn the tragedy of war - in the present as well as the past.

When he writes directly about his work as a judge Paul offers us rare insight into the hard labour of listening to difficult cases and coping with frustrating procedural structures and practice. The moments of protocol and pageantry that are also part and parcel of a judge's life are valued but sometimes lightly and self-deprecatingly mocked. And behind all of these duties and frustrations we hear the leitmotif of, words and doubts (...) woes and care, the daily background music of humanity against which a judge must seek to retain an openness to the occasional kind surprise.

The one constant and unambiguous source of comfort to be found throughout is the beneficence to be found in contemplation of the natural world in all its interacting elemental forms. It is a source of consolation, of surprise and pure sensuous pleasure whether in landscape where a trench in Picardy transforms itself over time into a velvet tunnel, or in the sensuous pleasures and challenges of weather, in Achill and Lough Eske for example. We are reminded to notice the changing faces of water under sun and sky and to recognise the power of a single flower, in this case the pansy, to bring grace and happiness to the darkest of days

And whether in the human or non-human world there is always colour. Paul's painter's eye and knowledge of pigment are put to use throughout the collection but perhaps nowhere more vividly than in the sonnet Rainbow Nation where the potential kaleidoscope of the spectrum is muddied only by failures of human aspiration.

And there is humour too! The comic side of many of these

serious topics is given free rein whether on the golf course, in observing the pretensions of great men or during an everyday visit to a barber's shop. Enjoy!

So thank you, Paul, for sharing this digest of a life energetically lived. You have taken us on a tour of times and places, people and ideas, and all with a sense of celebration of the joys of travel and exploration, of learning and - most importantly for this project perhaps - of poetry. We look forward to hearing more.

Some comments by Sir Reg Weir formerly a Lord Justice of Appeal in the Court of Appeal of Northern Ireland

With characteristic generosity of spirit, Paul has invited me to write something by way of an explanatory note to this volume of his poems illustrated by his paintings. I have been reticent about doing so because in truth I am an imposter in the role. Any such note should by rights be penned by our former and distinguished mutual judicial colleague, Sir Michael Nicholson. For Michael was the catalyst not only for the poems in this collection but for the very nascence of Paul as a poet.

In his introduction you will have seen Paul explain how his interest in writing poetry was incubated by the challenge that Michael delivered to all his then colleagues as we sat around the lunch table To our shame, nobody but Paul rose to that challenge. I should explain that in their downtime judges are no different from any other group of workers. They gossip, exchange jokes, laugh and tell stories on many topics that are sometimes connected but often far removed from the serious nature of their daily work. In short they let their hair down during that leisure time and their mental health is all the better for it.

That background sets the scene because, having once risen to Michael's challenge, Paul's enthusiasm for the medium of poetry developed by leaps and bounds. The many topics and themes discussed around the daily lunch table were on many of those days distilled by Paul within an hour into an apposite poem and promptly circulated amongst us to our invariable wonderment and delight.

Thus, over time was a considerable body of work assembled. My small part was, without having been asked and indeed without the knowledge of the poet, to print off most of the poems as they arrived and add a handwritten note so as to be able to recall what discussion had inspired the particular lines. I collected these and only years later did I mention to Paul that I had kept them. He thereupon borrowed my file and I am pleased to see that some have found their way into the present anthology. Michael was indeed the moving spirit though I am proud to have become his humble bag carrier. I hope that these poems will afford as much pleasure to those who are new to Paul's work as his fellow colleagues derived from those that he originally penned only for us.

CONTENTS

A sense of time and place

A Sense of Humour

A Sense of Judgment

A Sense of Tragedy

A sense of occasion

A sense of Romance

A sense of an ending

A SENSE OF TIME AND PLACE

Florentine Dawn

Red Medici ball, the sun upslips, upslides,
back lights in pink etched churches' domes
palazzo walls, suffused in light, now echoing
not yet the sounds of tramping tourist feet
but sounds of armoured ghosts, the clash of arms,
the rustling of Renaissance silks, unsheathing swords,
dark whispering condottieri, mad Pazzi
lusting for blood to spill on duomo's floor

while in Giotto's tower the campanone tolls.

In market, sun uplit, a jumble of empty boxes,
evokes that smoking, bonfired pile of vanities;
accursèd Savonarol' dark cursing still
as cynic serpent Machiavel' drips poison
into the ears of dukes, princes, prelates;
fat, flatulent Leo, the butt of Luther's wrath,
bestrides his horse along the muddy Arno's banks
while coins of gold tinkle into banker's hands

while in Giotto's tower the campanone tolls.

Still climbs the sun seeking its zenith
building its furnace heat and wilting
the drummed-out whispers from the past,
those sounds of tramping tourist feet
sun stripping the ancient peeling paint
sun melting the old-time jingling coins
sun burning up the ancient vanities
yet past is present - it is not gone

still in Giotto's tower the campanone tolls.

Lough Eske

First in the rain, Donegal dull drizzling dreich,
unbleached an old net curtain hangs on the lake
rent here and there enough for glimmers of light
to break upon the sleeping water, demisting slight,
dappling and daubing lit luminous shards
giving the semblance of a life to a mirror,
misty brume containing the pearly promise
of a coming revelation, resurrection of hope.

Next day it comes with clarity, such clarity
aside are cast the dingy garb, the leaden gloom
azure against the stretching fingers of trees
branches bracken bracts and rampant reeds
birds flying flittering, a cumulus of clouds
and curly locks of hair the cirrus overhead
reflecting all, still unrefracting waters.

Samarkand

Not borne by djinnis on a Persian silken rug
we arrived on a train, a trundling train,
that shook its way across the Central Asian wastes
from Turkman Ashgabat, weird marble city,
figment of a despot's mind, yet realised,
white tombstone blocks, empty of souls.
The omnipresent president stares down
while cuddly laughing dogs he strokes.

We cross dull desiccated desert lands,
the untold wealth the oils and gas beneath
into Uzbeks' empty lands- more limbo sands,
punctuated by madrassas, mosques, minarets,
tiled turquoise, cobalt blue and emerald green,
shimmering invitations to the Paradise beyond.
Bukhara and Khiva, harems, pools, slave markets
echoing still to the sound of murderous lash.

To Samarkand, the jewel box of Tamerlane,
Temur the Lame lying still in his golden tomb,
forgotten now the rivers of blood he spilled
sating the parched thirsty desert spoil and grit,
folk hero smiles benign on brides and grooms
dispensing a blessing, that idol's fingers.
Cruelty forgiven and tyranny forgot, absolved,
Bad bloody history seen through tinted lens.

And then we come to Registan that square
Vast Heaven's antechamber, the gate of glory,
Pillars, domes, pilasters, its porticoes ablaze,
all soaring high, all richly iridescent lit,
sumptious as a rainbow turned to stone
shrinking us down to seeming tiny fleas
scurrying within kaleidoscope spellbound
beauty casting its veil on evils of the past.

San Gimignano

Ah
San Gimignano
old Manhattan
on Tuscan hill
pride strutting
brag of towers
sky scraping
so proud before
the fall of earls
counts princes
built on rocks
but yet on sand
slowly seeping
history tumbling into a*dvancing years* ***turning to romantic tales***
towers fallen - yet s*tanding- the abode of* ***gold tressed Rapunzels***
letting down their hair - now no handsome princes left to climb
through eyeless empty windows looked at but blankly staring
all is turned to dizzying dislocating Disney world of faux fairies
spaghetti vongole tomatoes the colour of blood no longer spilled
the clash of knives and forks but *not of sharpened daggers drawn*
the setting sun kissing again San Gimignano - the sleeping beauty.
....

The Camino

Spangled scintillas, stars all strung,
Galician gems in a galaxy hung,
glittering gold in the black of night
opening the Way and giving a light
for a rock at sea and sailing afloat
bones of a saint in a stone made boat.

St Jacques, Santiago or simply James,
an apostle of peace with many names
comes not as a dove, now Slayer of Moors,
warrior Mars with his swords and his cures.
Pilgrims they came in a stream then a flood
blisters snow-bitten, boots covered in mud.

Consciences cleansed by a scallop shell
reaching for heaven and dodging hell,
in through the Pòrtica, their faith intense
sanctity's odours on clouds of incense.
That star-studded myth, it still holds sway,
the pilgrims still come, still walk the Way.

A stone boat at sea, it cannot be real
a legend, a story, a traveller's tall tale?
What is the lure and what is the draw?
It can't be that boat that nobody saw.
Follow those stars, the wayfarer's goal
To lift up his heart, rediscover his soul.

In the Garden of Good and Evil

Two arms embrace two lakes   turquoise on silk
Belpaese's true delight that garden paradise
where sun flung diamonds gleam and glint
Lecco Lake and Como shimmer join and meld
where once Bethrothed there walked and kissed
Rodrigo's evil clutches fled   that devil Don
here blue waters lick and gentle lap serene
the Villa Monastero's slopes all verdant green.

I came with easel brush and paints to stand
imbibe the Alps majestic soaring magic grand
see plants arrayed in coloured serried banks
jag leaved upstretching shrubs soft leavèd trees
quivering in that italic balmy passing breeze
a convent garden once it was now long displaced
expelled those fallen sisters lustful lewd disgraced
by lives of broken vows and lies exiled erased.

As there I quiet watched and drank all deeply in
came rustle from a shaded spine leaved pine
long languorous slithering slimy green it slid
a snake that stopped and greedy eyed its prey
it raised its head grew still and cold eyed stared
then fork tongued struck and sated belly crawled
back through dead and dusty crackling leaves.
Spell broken Paradise re-lost old Eden's tale reprised.

The Garden of the Villa Monastero is one of the most beautiful gardens of Italy. It overlooks Lakes Lecco and Como. It was originally the site of a nunnery. The decadence of the nuns and their dwindling numbers led to its closure. The area forms the backdrop to Manzoni's great novel The Betrothed a tale of two young lovers whose marriage the evil Don Rodrigo sets out to prevent. Manzoni's sister married into the family who owned the lands.

Starlings over St Peter's

Portentous pious impious   all soaring high
indulgence built on stone   pilastered pride
colonnades of columns   carved pillars to the sky
the piazza go across and the rising steps you climb
through portal doors you go to see a sight sublime

O'er mortal heads a-spin overwhelms a vault that looms
Bernini's baldacchino naves altars gold and tombs
white polished peerless Pietà Carrara pure and sad
stands bullet proofed in glass against a hammer mad
where heaven-gawping tourists stand in crowds and stare.

They mutter beaded prayers or idle gossip share
they feel the touch of angels' wings that beat upon the air
engaged in unseen war with demon bats baroque
invisible but black   who endless spit and mock
on singing saints who pray and praise all faithful still.

Berretto-ed scarlet clerics some black enough to kill
in twisted hands stilettos cut and slash and stab
you shiver in the chill of wolves who holy treasures grab
libidinous the Borgias whose loot those thieves befits
enwrapped in golden capes great Dante's hypocrites.

Shake from your back those devils just onward stride
heavenwards then move   go up that dome inside
up spiralling you step   low bend along the side
emerge to twilight evening the dusk all peachy pinks
behold the sun that lights an empire's ruins then sinks.

Look out across disciples' heads dead frozen into stone
and watch a murmuration a black lace mantilla blown
that dives, then climbs, it shrinks, comes flying back regrown
no rigid lines or dogmas here this game of light and shade
just simply freedom's joy redeemed and endlessly replayed.

Kings College Chapel

+ +
xxx xxx
xxxxx A xxxxx
xxxxx Cam mist xxxxx
xxxxx river's even exhalation xxxxx
xxxxx towers loom dissolve in fog xxxxx
xxxxx street lamps with haloes glow xxxxx
escutcheoned gates down lit black iron wrought
from college Clare to tragic Henry's church I go
gone gothic lines of daylight's stone carved lace
by darkness smudged all sepia umber running ink
great darkling window mere dimly etched outlined
as diffident through door ajar at side within I step
part see a jewel box where glass cased candles gleam
illuminating hint of lustrous gilded chiselled walls
on high above a vaulted honeycomb of roof afloat
sonority on wings of reverent choir reverberates
tenor baritone and bass descants cascade descend
sounds swell and rivers flow on heaven's harmony
frozen a moment of time to eternal turns ephemeral
light dark sounds silenced last hymn to a dying day
the promise of new life the coming light of dawn
to flow across the coloured slivers of melted glass
transform that shadow window dim and show in full
true glory of doomed Henry's priceless gift to God.

Mussenden Temple

Mussenden Temple was built as a library beside his palatial home by the Earl Bishop Harvey Bishop of Derry and Earl of Bristol at Downhill on the Northern Ireland Atlantic coast atop a cliff. A bon viveur non-believer he travelled around Europe the namesake of many Bristol Hotels.

Mussenden Sunset

we
cross the lea
evening umbered
steps crush the grass
sheep marbles missed
to house of the Yeatsian stare
not burned for freedom in a fight
defenstered eyes gouged out by thieves
to Derry's Montorio tempietto once house of books
set on a cliff of rock o'er ever rodent rising waves
the petrine gift to Frideswide's beauty stands erect
against a sky of gold uplit and hued in violet pink
moist cottonwool the laden Heaven's moving mists
in eventide turned evanescent lambent polychrome
ephemera afloat transformed to vision of eternal truth
a mise en scène limelit the beams they flow and pool
in luminescent ponds of light on north Atlantic's seas
a picture from a childhood bible tale those godly rays
searchlights crepuscular the piercing shafts of a God
the doubting sybarite a bishop served not nor loved
flamboyant and extravagant traipsing and stravaiging
from gilded salon to tiled salotto, from Rome to Paris
eyes cast not at paradise aloft but reflected in a sherry
funds flow free sweet syrup of plantation Carib sweat
around that dome ironic poet's Latin words inscribed
Pleasant indeed it is to gaze upon another's work and toil

xxxxxxx
xxxxxxx

SKELLIG MICHAEL

A
grey
splinter
of bare rock
white foam footed
skyward steep ascends
Atlantic ocean's bastion spire
pointing to heaven's sombre silver
we land we mount on foot those steps
e climb that endless stairway open spiral
another Jacob's ladder angels now unseen
gargoyles that glint in sandstone and in slate
we cross Christ's slight green saddle and touch
the heathered stones where sea pinks cling and smile
no busy bees buzzing now to fill those hill-top hives
gone bees of the invisible the monks who gathered nectar
made honey in stone desert gardens for their thirsty souls
and all the while great gangling gannets, gulls and guillemots
circling spin and plaintive sad they cry reel wheel and whine
if still guides the sailor's way the lighthouse on that rock
do gather still and taste true honey our storm tossed souls?
xxxxxxxxxxxxxxxxxxxxxxxxxxxxxxxxxxxxxxxxxxxxxxxxxxxxxxxxxxxxxxxxxxxxxxxxxxxxxx
xxxxxxxxxxxxxxxxxxxxxxxxxxxxxxxxxxxxxxxxxxxxxxxxxxxxxxxxxxxxxxxxxxxxxxxxxxxxxx
xxxxxxx xxxxxxxxxx xxxxxxxxxxxx xxxxxxxxxx xxxxxxxxxxxxxxxxxxxxxxxxxxxxxxxxx

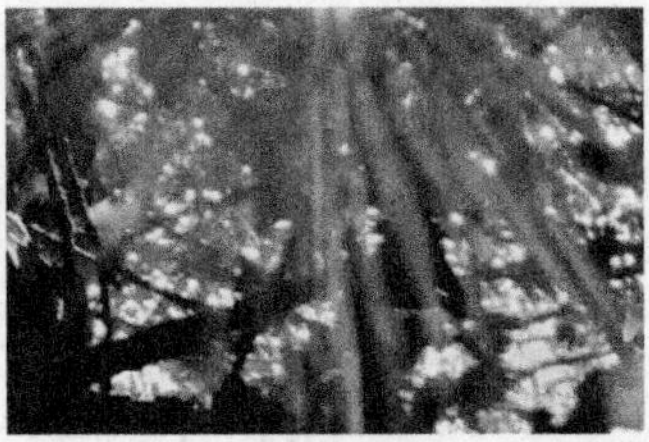

In Drumnamh Wood
Slua na Sí – The Fairy Host

breeze kisses rustling leaves
fingers tinkle twitched chimes
light dapples in luminous dene
bright sprinkles of white
on brown earth grass green

through canopied quivering leaves
twigs etch tree-lace on the sky
sun shafts through the branches
a prism rich as a rainbow high
up-down-heavenwards rays flow

fairies in frolics beguiling glow
fées hovering glittering all at play
mix mischievous magic and lore
beckon and flitter and flutter away
up through the beams and the tree

enchantment aloft of *slua na sí.*

Slua na sí (pronounced slewa na shee): the fairy host (Irish)
Fées (pronounced fay): fairies (French)

In Drumnamh Wood
I nDroim nDamh

Nine years in war they silent witness stand
verdant youths in spring in autumn dying gold
summer's rustling robes all murmurous green
the dagger tears of winter's drip-dripping ice
encircling ferny raths of old the derry turns
hiding place for Gaelic gallowglass and kern.

Nine years in war they stand and silent watch
sly eyes peek round the solid ivied trunks
heads severed off and bloody bodies fall
trees silent hear the burdened breath of men
heavy their armour-plated panoply of war
the screams, sobs, shouts of Gael and Gall.

When peace it comes earls fleeing Kin/sail
no peace for gentle innocents those oaks
wood cutters, sawyers, axe men axed and cut
holocaust of humble timber to bondage sold
hatchets hacked spliced planks that fall
new turned to gates in other Derry's wall.

If now you walk through Drumlamph Wood
and stand 'neath outstretched arms of oaks
remember victims of that war which we forgot
feel raindrops cold drip drop from leaves
hear echoed sylvan voices crossing years
those sobbing orphaned oaks, their tears.

Footnote

In 1593 Hugh O'Neill Earl Tyrone led a rebellion against Queen Elizabeth that started the Nine Year's War which ended in defeat in the Battle of Kinsale and the Flight of the Earls. Ulster was the scene of much of the war. The huge oaks forests in Ulster provided cover for rebel Gaelic kerns. Following the slaughter in that war Ulster was pacified and then planted under James I. Huge swathes of the great Ulster forests were felled and the wood used in the plantation and in the building of the English navy. Drumlamph Wood is a tiny remnant of what was once a mighty forest. The oak woods of Ireland are remembered in the word Derry (Doire in Irish).

Black and White

Vietnam *Washington DC*
remembered
black chiselled
into granite ice cold
unstoppable names flow
unhinged an abacus of death
marshalled in dread lines sons dead
turned to a heart-rending flow A to Z
and there out across the snow Korea's turn
combat accoutred warriors stand all darkly stern
congealed fixed staring soldiers their guns they tend
sweat blood and tears all turned icicles hard-frozen drip
stage sombre set for an unsung silent requiem in vestments black

Altamont Co Carlow

Beneath the soil terra firma's warriors toil peacekeeping troop
the snowdrop swords green leaves soft melt the frosts and ice
hinged humble hanging heads they bow and stoop and droop
messengers immaculate of spring enlightenment to come
shed ice-touched tears that unseen gentle flow
shiver still and soft stand in milky snow
side sombre yews and grey graven tombs
o'er this platoon no hatred looms
strewn once on abbey altars
for cold winter's end
at Candlemas
so pure so
white.

The Vietnam Veterans memorial in Washington DC is in a two-acre site dominated by two black granite walls engraved with the names of those service members who died or remain missing in the war in Vietnam. In the Korean War memorial on the other side of the park there are 19 stainless steel statues collectively called the Column the figures represent a platoon on patrol. All are dressed in full combat gear dispersed among strips of granite and juniper bushes representing the rugged terrain of Korea. Seen in winter snow and ice they are a poignant sight.

Snowdrops (galanthus in Greek (literally the milk white plant) have been taken to represent chastity, death, consolation, purity and friendship. They were scattered on altars on Candlemas Day commemorating the presentation of Jesus at the Temple as the light of the world. A medicinal plant used by monks for the treatment of mal de tête galanthamine a chemical found in snowdrops is now used to treat Alzheimers. Altamont Garden in Co Carlow has one of the finest collections of snowdrops in Ireland.

Pandemia

Tramonto nell'ovest con i nubi in feste
E cielo sereno, che bellezza celeste!
Colori stupendi - grigiastri, rosastri,
Che risposta di gioia a tanti disastri.
Come cuscini di neve, di cotone idrofilo
Braccia di luce, un pezzo ombrofilo
Un raggio di sole che taglia i nubi,
Scaccia i sogni, destrugge incubi
Cade nel mare con gran luce diffusa
E mucchi di nuvole alla rinfusa
Ma scende il sole ed ecco tenebre
Scura la notte, senza stelle, funebre
Son' chiuse le tende, son' chiuse le porte
Arriva la peste, arriva la morte?
Ma non è la fine, ritorna la luce
L'alba riviene, nuova speranza conduce.

Pandemic

West sets the sun the clouds all in fiesta
bright sky still in clear heaven celestial
fringed rosy and grey sky's colours amaze
an answer of joy in catastrophe's days
cotton wool pads like pillows of snow
through patches of dark lights still flow
cutting through clouds sun dying gleams
scattering nightmares chasing bad dreams
sea struck by light all bright and defused
clouds swirl and rise and billow confused
sun sinks sky darkens then all is aethereal
now starless and black dark night funereal
curtains are drawn we shut all our doors
pandemic or death - what's lurking in store?
Bright light will return   we're not at the end
coming dawn light   new hope will resend.

Achill

Two Bays Two Days

In memory of John Murray former Chief Justice of Ireland, Judge of the European Court of Justice and friend

Battleship grey the sky leaden
great minotaur Minaun's floating back
looms its cliffs turn gloomy black
and all the while inward accoutred pluming
sea knights breakers tall white spumed
incoming endless crash, break and fall
pour viscous silver on wettened sand
on Trawmore Trá Mór that great strand.
With John we go those knights to fight
heavens darkening more we dive and swim
cold water thrown on faces and we feel
exhilaration in the waters down at Keel.

An Achill sunlit day blue sky-ed
so out over clifftop road we ride
and see it nestling there, the strand
tween Moyteoge Head and great Croghaun
colours today high lit, gold vibrant sand
the greys and blacks of yesterday have gone
sea turquoise painted greens and blues
fraying gently on the beach in ones and twos
waves that lap don't crash or break or fall
the waters beckon and kind mermaids call
no banshees here rather an angel's dream
with John we swim in water silk at Keem.

FAREWELL TO TURF

memories unlocked not by new ground coffee beans
or bacon sizzling in a pan or by Proust's madeleine
but by circling swirls of turf fresh burned
clinging to the tweedy fabric of the western world
secular incense that flows from chimney thuribles
sliced like chocolate brownies from yielding earth
stacked earthen lumps built up like Irish pyramids
left out to dry beneath the grey and leaden skies
high piled creel carried waiting for sparks and flames
to set free those scented spectres from the past
poignant puncturing stabs of unforgetting grief
homes tumbled ships laden those tears so bitter wept
poor man's brown coal that burns to whitened ash
transubstanced emptiness from seeming solid earth
gone up in smoke leaving more than a hint of a scent
hanging in the air like a long lingering farewell
now burning out those fires slán leat a mhóin a chara

slán leat a chara ; farewell friend

Sarees

In Agra's streets in brown and grey manure
the gift of holy cows that wander free
disturbing sight for westerners to see
who see in cleanliness life's second cure.

They onward push and shove, that crowd,
beggars here and vendors there who shout.
Pots, pans, bright fruits, red chilli pods they tout
while holy men ash faced cry prayers aloud.

An unlimbed child   a mendicant thus made
holds out a single begging hand for coins
while pocket pinching mother other cash purloins
the inequalities of life so harshly thus displayed.

Overwhelming Indian life in colour, sound and smell.
Those cycling hordes and battered cars that hoot,
poisonous lorries belching smoky fumes pollute.
Uplifting scenes mixed up with ones from hell.

Balletic beauty sudden drifting past we see
three graces cross our path in silken sarees clad.
Each seems to float and each diaphanous dryad.
Manure untouched airborne they wander free.

La Salute Venice

Do we see
dream city waters mirror
imagine liquid refulgence infused confused
refraction reflected lingering lines blurred angles
soft touching kissing melded melting waters
responding pallets of pastel pink ochred tints
raw sienna burnt umbers Naples yellow
surfacing swimming and floating on sunlit exuberance
dissolving into moods and wisps of mournful mist?
Do we see strange masked spectres bubble up and leer
beckoning us into Casanova's masked world of courtesans
concerti played on plangent violins the *dances macabres*
of an age decaying the fall of an empire the end of times?
Stands la Salute still offering thanks for the end of a plague
that chameleon that ever changes form and lingers still.
Is it all a metaphor mixed like paints on a plate of linseed oil
art worked into stones splashed unto stucco a riot inspired
reality dreamt that lifted the dream and flung it
into the arms of the sea supposed bride
to wed a groom not now long since gone
faithless jaded sated by indulgence
yet recalling it all
sadly watching
the waters
rise.

Sojourn in Cortona, Umbria

For Reg and Carol generous hosts

Day 1

Up hairpin bends enough a saint to scare
we park our Fiat in brave Garibaldi's square
await our host and with a furtive eye
watch out for traffic cop in time to spy -
here comes she now   fair Botticelli in a cap
avert our gaze   pretend to read our map
and timely comes pink shirted welcome host
off speed we all and promptly clear the coast.

Down serpent twists our quickening race we make
past *cimitero's* grey and petrine wedding cake
and there upon our left and up we sudden see
a car park lined with logs unwanted from a tree
cancella opened wide   up stony steps we mount
expect to see a fish cascading water fount
but there before our eyes blue swimming pond
a garden manicured well stocked and lawned.

Plumbago sprouts from out a spout a gentle blue
and Carol careful comes on platform shoe
see now a *palazzino* built with grace and taste
all looks enchanting and everything in place
a poolside rosé wine expectantly we sip
though sickly petillance will disappoint our lip
but come there now some better wines instead
full bodied Chianti wines all strong and bloody red.

Into a sun drenched *cortile* we staggering go
prosciuttoed melon strips and wines that ever flow
dark aubergines and peppers with egg frittata mix
no end to Carol's skilful little kitchen tricks
and flustered fretting Reg himself gets in a flutter
must go retrieve a dish of sun melting yellow butter
and then we loudly hear the cutting of the lawn.
By whom? A passing satyr or a Bacchic faun?

We spy a hatted man a simple *giardiniere*
eccentric yes and tall and just a little scary
I try a little chat a bit of foreign intercourse
finds he my language baffling or fluent tour de force?
We eat our chocolate *baci* all melting in the sun
enwrapped in clichéed lines we have some fun
and wisely hoping now to miss postprandial slump
into the moving water of the pool I tipsy jump.

Day 2

Next day we see a group a Minnesotan clan
the woman ageing badly the man a cycling fan
their son is going to college to study anthropology
why not simply study a course of straight codology?
We talk of US cyclists of wheels and hilly starts
of cheats who stick on plasters to help their privy parts
down *strade cortonesi* slowly now we walk
through market stores we go and watch the sellers hawk.

We enter now town's Scala and see its serried seats
then out we come and see the city's other treats
see rows of *zii* upon Il Pozzo's wall
the scenes of Tuscan vineyards I truly love them all.
A stylish bar we enter its decor to admire
but large boobed painted ladies cannot inspire
back down to Garibaldi square our way we make
stare out across the plain to Trasimeno lake.

A belvedere besmirched by drug induced disgraces
that gives a view of Mary's Church of Many Graces
up hilly street we climb intent on lunch to find
pass *enoteche* crowded their tables carefully lined
bambino falls from bike with very noisy clatter
beside the stylish window of a sad unmarried hatter
find table in the shade in the Piazza Signorelli
lasagne antipasti and some porcini tagliatelle.

Escaping mounting *afa* the stifling sun and heat
to museum's scenes of Russia we gladly now retreat
see rows of chiaroscuro haunted Russian faces
white frozen steppes of ice and soulless wintry spaces
watched not by KGB in far away Archangel
but by a shapely blonde a Donatello angel.
On crumbling steps we sit and take a little rest
and looking around the scene by all we are impressed.

From archways hanging dangling we see some iron hooks
from where they hanged their traitors or simple thieving crooks
then Carol sees a waiter she thinks a Proustian man
I fail to see the likeness though striving best I can.
Is this because I see just the passing of his rear
black hair on neck and just a corner of an ear?
So back down to Sodo go and down we do descend
the day is nearly done the *vacanza* near its end.

Refrigerated baci and a timely cup of char
a fond farewell and kisses and then our sun-baked car.
Some things from out my mind I simply can't dispel
a scene from Dante's Paradise and one from out his Hell.
A picture in that stylish bar surreal and red
blood flowing upon a lady asleep upon a bed
all coming out a fan from eviscerated bat.
And from Il Paradiso? Fair Carol in her hat.

Cimitero- *cemetery* ***cancella*** *– gate* ***palazzino*** *– little palace* ***cortile-*** *court yard*
Giardiniere *– gardener* ***strade cortonesi*** *– streets of Cortona* ***zii*** *– old codgers*
Enoteche *- wine bars* ***afa*** *– oppressive sultriness* ***vacanza*** *– holiday*

Viole del pensiero nel tempo del Covid

Pansies pensées belle viole dei pensieri
non dei pensieri di noialtri prigionieri
non i pensieri cupi di quest' mondo strano
dove viviamo nella tristezza di quest'anno.

Sul viso di velluto che lieto sorriso!
pensiero di gioia sulla faccia inciso
che ricchi colori che dolci guance
non per loro le nostre funebri ciance.

se vi scoraggiate diventate depressi
se vi avvilite diventate oppressi
guardate i fiori vera opera di bene
dal paradiso immagini - belle tranquille serene.

Pansies in the time of Covid

Pansies pensées the fair viola's thoughts
not thoughts in prison cells unwished unsought
not dark thoughts we feel in dislocated world
where inward sadness flows in waves unfurled.

Uplifting see its smile on soft and velvet face
inscribed with joy imbued a face of melting grace
all beaming happiness up-lit and rich in colours
true antidote to Covid and all its baleful dolours.

If discouraged now and sore you feel depressed
if downhearted and in your very soul oppressed
contemplate that flower   true face of love
gentle and serene a gift from paradise above.

Pansy from the French pensée, a thought.

Wise Men

They came star gazing magi from somewhere in the east
on pilgrimage of faith or on a quest for truth at least
but did they come with turbans or wearing gilded crowns
on camel backs and wrapped in silken flowing gowns?

And did they come across the Arab dunes of sand
through starlit waving palms from out a distant land
and was one really black and were there only three
portrayed on glittering cards as usually we can see?

Lost in a fancy reliquary the message of that tale
seducing images of art a quite misleading trail.
The man in search of truth must surely quest
and kneel beside or near the light that's truly best.

Take not the gilded coins by tawdry bankers sold
but seek to bring to God the wise men's lasting gold.
Seek out the way of truth and find its loving sense
true meaning of that gold the myrrh and frankincence.

Let's ponder on the message of that ancient lay
the death of innocents another king did slay
yet still we hear in Ramah Rachel's rending cries
the cruelty of tyrants their evil and their lies.

Berlin Cathedral

Solid stolid cold looms
rock unforgiving block
cross topped dome in gloom
remembrance of Berlin's doom

inside beatitudes emblazoned
over gilded gawdiness below
here no meek nor poor   just show
a Kaiser's tomb and Kaiserin

Friedhof but one unstilled
no mourning touching tears
for terror of past victims' fears
the fields of peace untilled

no place this for the wise rabbi
who walked on holy ground
his kingdom cannot here be found
in this stone-built temple of irony.

Friedhof : a grave yard, literally a place of peace

Autumn in the New Forest

Along the path beech leaf strewn we walk
while camouflaged the dogs in bracken run
chase perhaps a fleeing rabbit's scent or hare's
dangling tongues betraying a canine sense of fun
while all the while the leaves they fall like flakes
a blizzard but not of white and chilling snow.

Those russet browns the yellows reds a gilded show
reflected all   in lake still waters seem to glow
autumn's light flows through trees their watery toes
upside down a world where mirrored beauty grows
birds flutter twitter tweet through upturned twigs
ungloving showgirl trees let fall their tinted wigs.

Leaf red its breast   tame robin with no cares
settled on a fungus sprouting trunk it cheeky stares
a sudden movement rustles in a nearby bush
red squirrels up a tree they run and rush
just a flash of bushy tail its hint we seem to see
disappearing into the innards of a tree.

Over leaves still crisp we trek and crunch
feel underfoot the crush of nuts the squirrels' lunch
hear soon a sudden snort a muffled neigh
put dogs on lead   they come New Forest ponies
soft nosed those three old long toothed cronies
soon wander off to munch a bale of summer's hay.

Our welcome woodland cottage at last we see
and savour thoughts of autumn apple pie for tea.

A Sense of Humour

Rough Luck

Taut, tense and stiff, teeing up new glistening ball
His club in doubtful hands and standing stiff
He fears a hook, expects a slice and then he hits
The spluttering ball descends and falls and sits.

In marram grass, unyielding sandy rough.
He tramps across the tufts, all golden tough,
And here he looks and there he throws a glance
But all he sees are harebells blue and all a-dance.

Seeks here and there and pokes through herbal wire
New ball is lost but upwards goes an avian flyer.
A wingèd lark, ascending answer to despond,
To golfer's gloom seeks songful to respond.

Celestial blue the sky, the nestling's holy goal
Though written off the golfer's goal, the hole.
Uplifted flies the bird as if to kiss the sun -
How much better this than hole in one.

A man with one eye on the past is wise. A man with two eyes on the past is blind.

These Years of Anniversaries

Let's mar our pleasant days no more
songbirds of passage those days of yore
catch at today   forget the days before
live in the present and leave old time lore.

All talk of anniversaries the ghosts of past
a pall upon our daily happy life will cast
let dust of ancient battles skirmishes and war
our throats no longer fill   our eyesight mar.

Nostalgia for the past forget   no longer pine
wait instead the opening of a bubbly tasty wine
and hidden in our past let's leave our roots
history drowned in sparkling champagne flutes.

The Anhedonist

He graceless sits - no hedonist - true Calvin's charmless son
Success without felicity   for him no sporting fun
not for him the pleasures of wee drams or cups
no effervescent taste buds a-dancing when he sups
with all the dreary glumness of a chilly lowland kirk
a sunless face that reeks of peaty smoke and murk.
Can ever he be challenged to wanly try to smile
or even try to laugh albeit in a Scottish kind of style?
But even cloudy eyes might give a Pictish twinkle
and down turned lips betray a half smiling little wrinkle
when grandson Jock climbs up upon his knee
and stares him in his eyes to see what he can see
and laughs aloud to see dour grandpa grin
when Jock pulled hard upon that Scottish hairy chin.

Anhedonia: the inability to experience pleasure

Last Cornetto

On plinth he stands   the Union's doughty fighter
to some a hero great   to some a pompous blighter
a *duce* to the orange men   to modern ears a bore
he glares across the hills towards nearby Strangford shore

on frowning face we see that dark messiah's stare
long nosed through nostrils wide he breathes the Belfast air
the balmy breeze it carries the scents from perfumed garden
the resolve of wilting man to strengthen and to harden

and back fly thoughts to Edith   Lady Londonderry's set
her boudoir and her tea-cups   her two-some têtes à têtes
he thinks of Edith's spouse   a wealthy man   that peer
whose portrait hangs in Queens commanding with a sneer

while Edith carried on   no hint of guilt portrayed
who kept the coal fires burning as she partied and she played
Great Edward stands all stony and frozen now in time
what see we on his arms - is that algae wet or slime?

in empty hand was something now disappeared and gone
a sword aloft in air or a torch that burned and shone?
it's not algae on his arms but a viscous kind of melt
no weapon from his scabbard imagined at his belt

Great Carson Man of Steel aloft a lump of stone
his *gelato* has all melted and gone his ice cream cone.

The Rainbow Nation

Red sails across the glorious Portstewart evening sky
sunsetting rays and orange, yellow hues on high
and Erin's emerald greens high-lit and set ablaze
Caerulean, phtalo, Prussian, cobalt blues amaze
on rising watery waves deep indigo in streaks
deep violet tones on distant Irish western peaks.
This land a painting book of myriad tones and shade
as like a palette for great minds and spirits made.
The fools the fools the fools no scholars here or saints
blind to the beauty of this land its wondrous natural paints.
Together stir the colours and act like silly clowns
turn everything to sludge to sickly dirty browns.
Our short sightedness we presbyopic flaunt.
A mish mash messy mix that's what we seem to want.

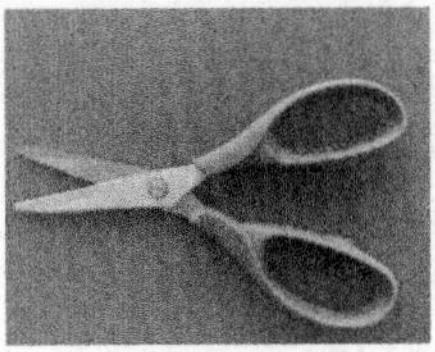

Unkindest Cut

This was the unkindest cut of all. Julius Caesar Act 3 Sc 2

Through Dublin streets he walks on route to barber shop
hirsute his head erect greying hairs ablaze on top
a younger son in tow who sports a fairer head
intent on rugby game he quickens up his tread.

The leader of the pack goes through the glassy door
he hopes that no delay will keep him from the score.
He envious watches son being led by girl away
and disappointed sees his barber's old and gray.

Now like proverbial lamb to cutting slaughter led
the tresses of a Sampson all severed from his head
he shivers under fingers that linger in his hair
the barber gaily cutting with style élan and flair.

When now the cutting's over at last the snipping's ceased.
the time has come to pay - to be well and truly fleeced.
How can you be so brazen? we hear him gently ask
Dick Turpin when he robbed you at least he wore a mask.

Fiscal Rectitude

Written in the time of the Euro Greek crisis. Times change!

Sweet Bechstein sounds, teutonic pianoforte tinkles
as over Fatherland the star of fortune twinkles.
Sleek BMWs roll out along the autobahns and purr
while Franz and Hans and Hanna start new European tour.

Beach towels all packed and ready for new occupations
they're on a pleasure march to southern bankrupt nations.
The serried ranks of beach chairs new ersatz tanks
fresh thrones again for those now risen up the ranks.

Those bulging wads of euros an unappealing sight
dispensed from pockets deep in lederhosen tight
remains of Graeco-Roman now broken and quite shattered
as Athens' hungry children in rags they beg all tattered.

An end to Bunga Bunga orgies to foul priapic beasts
an end to wasted pasta   vice driven drunken feasts.
Let them dance to a waltz or better still a marching tune
and let them rise at six and not lie in bed till noon.

See now them come, King Friedrich's kith and kin,
by work redeemed, they've grown a euro thickened skin
aloft they sit   adopt a wise and very seemly attitude
buoyed righteous up in new-found fiscal rectitude.

A case of déjà vu? All written in the stars or so they'd say.
So now belongs to them the morrow and today.
If Manzoni's Renzo listened by Lake Como or Lake Lecco
in Calabrese streets would old jackboots seem to echo?

Café de l'Absinthe

Inspired by Degas' masterpiece in the Musée d'Orsay

Sad eyed she sits and stares across the passing years
And see we from her lashes emerging salty tears?
Ensconced among the smoke in the Café de l'Absinthe
Has she discovered her partner's really mean and skint?

And who's the whiskered man beside her looking left
is he her erstwhile lover boy who's left her now bereft?
Or seeks she in the café a would-be client for the night?
The sadness of her face would put any man to flight.

Or is she a musing thinker a would-be philosophe
A poetess at work who's thinking out a strophe?
A travelling legal expert bemused by foreign laws
who contemplates reflective a foreign system's flaws?

My mind is far too active and now I simply think
She's just a tired young woman who's ready for a drink.

Reflections on the Eve of Trafalgar Day 21 October

On attaining 60 on 20 October 2008

Now over the hill I'm a sexagenarian bemused
freed from youth's chains by champagne infused

rigid conventions dispelled and away I am free
uncensored my ears   wide eyed I shall see

life in its comedy   smile's curve on my lips
like old Dublin's councillors the bubbly I'll sip

and hear Shavian tale of Major Barbara's tryst
of wine swilling judges playing with the list

intrepid as Hotspur I'll become a young Harry
dispense with armed mail no baggage I'll carry

like Nelson blind eye to dangers I'll show
cannonballs of fortune just scornful I'll throw

with old age or worse if thrown on the deck
just leave me alone   keep Hardy in check.

Trouble up't Mill

Boulevard de Clichy Paris   Moulin Rouge red mill
hirsute and stylish boulevardiers with time to kill
they come to sup a while and feast their wondering eyes
on sequined tights those ruffled skirts and thighs.

See nubile girls on swings above their tables high
all lightly clad and angel like they seem to fly
they tap to the tunes their feet in shoes of crocodile
and add to the place a louche and creepy style.

Cloaque de tous les vices sans the usual awful smell
that lingers round a place like this   if truth we tell.

Perhaps we need to find a cleaner fresher place
a land of pure undriven snow and virgin space
no fleshpots there but only simple rustic stews
no *boïtes de nuit* ennui alluring girls or booze.

No canapés or champagne flutes so full of cheer
just simple wholesome pies and English ale and beer
though some might think that place just dull and dead
and long for another night in Place Pigalle instead.

Another Irish Airman foresees his Death

Off to the airfield he rushing goes intent on flight
across his piercing eyes pulls down his goggles
he climbs across the wings intent on aviator might
in cockpit climbs and manful fiddles with his toggles.

Imagines he's an airman ace against the cruel Boche
he'd set alive the engines and check his airman's gun
and drunk on lure of Messerschmitts and such like other tosh
all fearless crazed by thought of killing heathen Hun.

A leather covered helmet pulled down across his ears
he'd engine pedals feel through macho booted toes
a hero in his lunchtime undogged by women's fears
with silken handkerchief he'd loudly blow his nose.

Impassioned by that ancient *dulce et decorum* lie
for death and glory eager now and ready to be gone
but there behind broad shouldered back he hears a sigh
"Oh, do grow up" says Claire "just sit beside me, John."

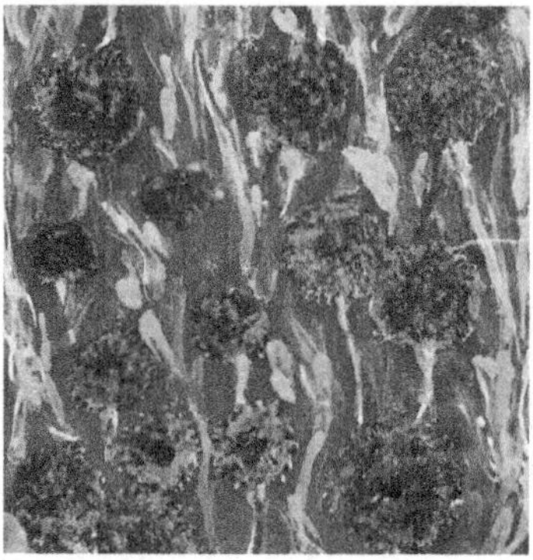

A-mused B-mused

The cornfields of my mind bare cut by sickle
now gone my muse, in favours promiscuous and fickle.
No more she strokes my head or whispers in my ear
the poet's empty now   bereft and uninspired, I fear.

No more she turns to waspish verse heard words of talk
or wrestles rhyming couplets that, yes, might shock.
Where treads that wraith-like spectre now, that lass?
Flown off to different shores on beating wings, alas.

Why flit she far away - inflation or the banking crash?
Dispelled by passing worries or sight of dwindling cash?
Or sadly washed away by endless summer rains
clutching her posies Ophelia-like down dripping drains?

Perhaps the ageing of the poet brings forth a kind of doom
the sense of verse and fun cut short by darkening gloom.
The ticking of the clock brings forward now his many years
with all their serried ranks of stalking age-filled fears.

Or else the absence of good triggers from mealtime talk
that once inspired those verses full of mirth and mock.
Methinks the poet needs on stubble field new seed
to bring again the flighty muse, entice and gently feed.

So, gently coax that missing muse - be yet so very kind
to cast abroad new seeds to fill the cornfields of my mind
and maybe soon we'll see again fresh bowers new
and cornfields lit by sun awash with corn flowers blue.

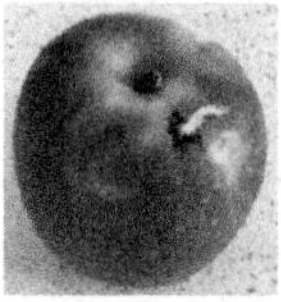

Answers given by some school children in a quiz:

Adam and Eve were created from an apple tree.

The Greeks were highly sculptured people and without them we would not have had history. The Greeks also had myths. A myth is female moth.

The Moth

Lepidopter daughter of an apple the mother of a killer
not tempted by a serpent snake but by a caterpillar
the source of all our sin and strife, progenitor of crime
floats wingèd in the air   flying o'er fields of time.

Homeric or Socratic well-honed and sculpted Greeks,
on Sarah's desert dunes dish-dashed the Muslim sheikhs
and Latin legions armed and, on the move, all roaming
face Goths and Visigoths in coming evening gloaming.

A giggling Brutus stabs a luckless dying Caesar
Mark Anthony takes ears and plays the rabble pleaser.
Lead poisoned and insane the truly loathsome Nero
tortures Romans with his fiddle   fails dismal as a hero.

From streets of Orleans rise the smells of frying steak
the chips are down for Joan aloft her burning stake
and armour-plated Bess with her stomach of a king
against the sleazy Spanish her sailing ships will fling.

Puts paid to Spaniard foe an English bowling skipper
who sails the English seas in his circumcising clipper.
In fair Verona's town Will Shakespeare in a doublet
searches for sweet Juliet an apt and rhyming couplet.

Napoleon flung by catapult to glory, power and fame
married a childless baroness what infamy, what shame!
With Darwin's specious origin comes end to holy feasts
'tween him and brother Marx the tide of faith retreats.

But history never died, with that Archducal assignation
came destruction and came doom to every western nation.
Where next that moth afloat   that giant female myth
that mother of the world   of all our kin and kith?

Had Tell's arrow missed the apple and hit the mythic head
Would our universe be spotless, a sinless place instead?

Destressing

No longer strive ambitious for perfection
be in be in the job of work deflection
in ergonomic comfort seated on your rump
think on things to wisely delegate and dump.

Well seated in your very comfy chairs
Offload all useless thoughts all worldly cares
and fiddling on computer's little knobs
just quiet sift away demanding papers, jobs.

No longer garner files to hold and hoard
You'll find the key on that key-board
unstress your fingers on that mouse and press
delete delete an end to work and stress.

Throw away your biro pens take up quills
seek no more the comfort of a drink or pills
concentrate instead upon the comfort of your feet
the angle of your back, your neck, your seat.

Check the way you use your eyes, your sight
get the angle of your writing wrist just right
worry not about old tension in your bones
deafly turn an ear to ringing mobile phones.

Let gently hypertension fall relax and ease
(and don't think that that's a new disease)
avoid all new and different types of stress
the answer is to write a poem and just do less.

The Servants of the Servants of God

Down mediaeval cloistered corridor there comes
a crowd of mitred bishops, girdles round fat tums,
all decked out in coloured robes of silk and sable
to sit around monks' simple Christian table.

They view askance chipped pots, cracked plates
they shiver at the thought of poor monastic fates.
Bishops plump, content, well fed, complacent
would surely miss their jewelled cups renascent.

A bishop portly priest his *pater nosters* hums
but still looks down his nose at beggars' crumbs.
Ere bishops lift their knives and forks or take a bite
There comes a dreadful, fear inspiring sight.

A beggar woman and her starving hungry son
through cloistered window see bishops' noisy fun.
A scene like that a bishop's appetite should kill
Should make his knife and fork grow still.

Pareidolia

Escape despair and find the cure for melancholia
go tablet free - take up the joys of pareidolia!
See hairy scary bears in clouds on high
smoke-breathing dragons waltz across the sky
with cuddly lambs and sheep in woolly coat
on brooms across the heavens witches float.

See lumbering shapes of spraying whales
contorted contoured pig-like face of Wales
long lines across the blue from tails of planes
the rising wraiths of smoke from chugging trains
strange visage brown and burnt a piece of toast
is that St Patrick's face or just a crispy ghost?

Ladies in their hats and gents with caps
white bearded man a Santa Claus perhaps?
Thin wizened guys long haired with smiles
they're just beach rack spread out in piles
black specks of mould on tiles turn into hares
become a spider which long-leggèd scares.

Or what's that we see a slug or snail?
tea leaves on sides of cups that tell a tale
a seeping creeping petrol splash once seen
takes on the hue of rainbow coloured sheen
or drop tomato ketchup with a splash
red speckles on the floor that's now a rash.

White snowy peaked fresh whipped ice cream
brings back our childhood Christmas dream.
Is that a plastic bag we see in flowering bed
it sudden seems a charming plant instead.
lichen gold and white on standing stones
forms picture of a goat or dried out bones.

A long horse face emerges from tree bark
chiaroscuro interplay of light and dark
a rain filled roadside puddle it can make
a sunny twinkling tree reflecting lake.
Shadows lit by sun on ground can fall
or dance like Banksy lines across a wall.

Imagination's wondrous products rich arrayed
in playground of your mind so well displayed.

Pareidolia is the instinctive behaviour of the human brain to ascribe familiar concepts to random objects. What do you see is this picture?

The tentative subjunctive

Would that subjunctive's soft subtle sound
were still in vogue and still be found
peppering our words with gentle insinuation
would that it had not gone on long vacation
kinder than indicative at times so clipped
would that still out British mouths it tripped
could we but find for it far better use
take from imperative its sounding harsh abuse
more clever than conditional words their ifs and buts
less certain than the future which tricks us into ruts
certainty of things to come impossible to see
could we but mother tongue's descent escape and flee.

Would that we could stop turning *you* to *youse*
the Anglo-Saxon goodly *ye* turned woolly ewes
why are we now on chairs just sadly glumly sat?
that sounds prosaic ill-mannered maybe even fat
could we not yet again on seats and chairs just sit
or use the present participles that justly fit?
whoever saw sat president or saw sat duck
let's rehabilitate old word stood or simply chuck
were you to change a standing stone to stood stone
that would jar would be quite against the tone
would that standing by the door you'd forebear to say
you're stood for that bad education should betray.

Would that no-one cut our words to shreds insist
we marshal acronyms in lines   please do desist
UVF SF PIRA   poor DHSS
initials severed hacked a mangled verbal mess
would that past tense's words were truly fun
and not excruciating words like seen and done
could we but grammar's tools reread relearn
and on our bendèd knees devout and hopeful yearn
that Kingdom of King's English come back return
would that we could the gloried lustre buff up reshine
refill our heads with words refined repolished fine
and hear again the flow of words well spoken clear
that ink-dripped from the pen of great Shakespeare.

i

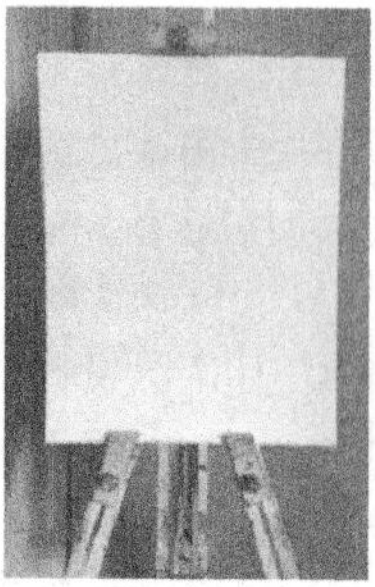

A Blank Canvas

A Danish artist who submitted empty frames as artwork told to repay funding

Blank canvas stretches out   unfolds
all virgin white   no pictured stories told
no lines awry   no painted spatters
to hurt our eyes   display extrinsic matters
possibilities flow undriven   like fresh snow
a void to let imagination soar and grow
where we can see what we desire
set our spirits and our eyes on fire
impress our minds with quivering leaves
poppies strewn on fields of sheaves
sunflowers that smile and twist and dance
horses passing by that jump and prance
imagined drops from paint filled pots
pointillism's marching ranks of little dots
mists hanging over pink tinted towers
flowers in drifts and rose filled bowers
sphinx-like eyes and enigmatic smile
angels flying high   rococo in their style.

No soulless empty canvas this   unfurled
A transcendental window to an artist's world.

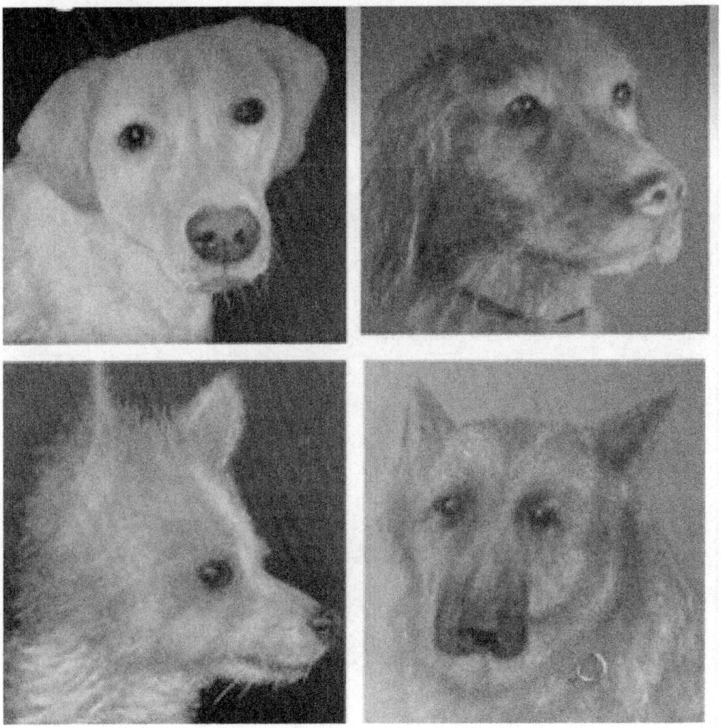

Rogan and Chara

Canine Delight

Unleashed they run across the strand
kicking up the golden piles of sand
unbounded hounds race towards the sea
through wiry grass both boundless free.

Up sand hill slopes some low some steep
through prickly clumps they jump and leap
then back to the frothy waves they tear
there stand stock still and sniffing stare.

Throw a ball and that they'll wildly chase
watch and see who's got the faster pace
they sudden stop slow down their speed
go off and chew some fresh seaweed.

Picking up a scent they wag their tail
aimless follow new wild goose trail
or let it go and pointless rush and roam
back to the salt filled spume and foam.

Nosey tongued sea watery salt imbibe
back to their mistress for a biscuit bribe
then off to a standing post to piddle
or run to jetsam snuffle sniff and widdle.

Back panting come they heed the call
slow down and stop and drop the ball
back on the lead now freedom's done
their day on the beach ~ what canine fun.

Puppets on a string

What if Eve had not listened to the snake
ignored the lure of knowledge's cursèd tree
would we be gardeners   happy naked free
if she did not that poisoned apple take?

Had Cleopatra had a truly ugly nose or face
and had not seduced Mark Anthony with charm
would he have missed sad fall from grace
would she have missed snake bitten harm?

If Bonaparte had been a handsome man and tall
would he have spent his time with girls not war
would he have turned deaf ear to Russia's call
not found his end in Saint Helena distant far?

If Hitler's gran had been kinder and more wise
would we've escaped that tyrant grim
not seen moustached that face   mesmeric eyes
not seen the world in flames   his insane whim?

Where go our lives   mere game mere dance?
Will we be led by love or cut adrift by hate?
Happy blessed our lives or victims of mischance?
Are we mere puppets on the strings of fate?

A Sense of Judgment

If thou be a severe, sour complexioned man then I disallow thee to be a competent judge.

The Compleat Angler   Izaak Walton

Bonfire of the Vanities
or
The Curse of the Photocopier

Yet still there come the trolley loads of wanton files
that groan and burst those paginated photocopied piles
black sombre tomes they're paginated yes digested no
a cartographic blizzard that lacks the charm of virgin snow.

They come young men and young girls too all sweating hot
the task of trundling boxloads to the court their tragic lot.
Impressive looking boxes come all tightly packed
files bulging very fat all common sense they lacked.

The product of long hours atop a greedy warm machine
where half asleep bamboozled clerks quite aimless lean
and out they come and flow the pages in a frenzied heat
a burden for the judge for those who charge a fee a treat.

No better place for them than bonfire burning bright
destruction of those vanities a longed-for worthwhile sight
and who'll this heresy destroy, who'll stoke the mighty fire
consign the worthless rubbish to its proper funeral pyre?

Come new born Savanarola this monster now to tame
consign this modern scourge to fires of hell and flame!

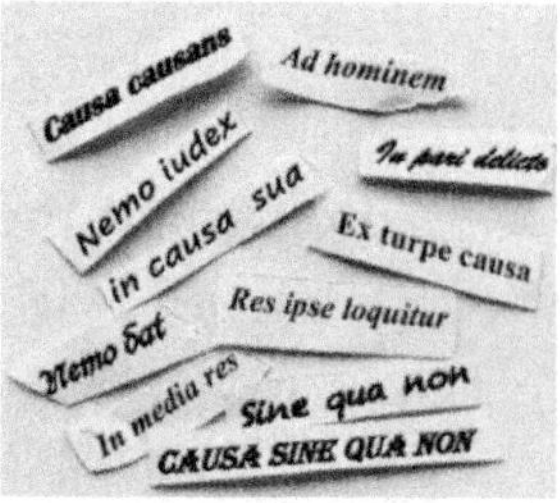

The Death of Legal Latin

Hearken to the bells that toll and clocks that chime
fast Doomsday comes, it's nearly judgement time.
To judge those misdemeanours, felonies and crime
what better way than versify with words that rhyme.

How can you find the proper thing to say, m'lud
dig with a pen like Heaney just find your spud.
Belles lettres scan and write with grace and flair
Mots justes from *Fleurs du Mal,* sweet Baudelaire.

Try *terze rime* alla Dante, great Iacopo da Todi,
or Chaucer's rustic words but avoid the very bawdy
or go with Mephistopheles that Goethe's Faustian pact.
Turn judgments into flowing works of art in fact.

But Latin? No! Today it's not *pari in materia*
those Roman words can now cause wild hysteria.
Non-classicists or monoglots one thing will surely tell
the modern Latinist is nothing but a ne'er do well.

Mention *pro bono* and lawyers become quite snappy
but a *magnum* of champagne still makes them very happy!

Pari in materia – relevant

The Circus is coming to Town

On the occasion of a visit by Law Lords to Belfast

With noses glued to panes to watch the circus come
we gleeful children wait, our mouths agape struck dumb
like Jesus' virgins wise await our bridegrooms decked
descended from far London, the peerless God's elect.

We listen to the roll of distant beat of drum
angels pull on strings and harps they pluck and strum.
Behold the caravans, along the road they trundle
in each a worthy lord, in each a legal bundle.

A cataract cascading of judgments, words and pages,
true lions of the mind, entrapped in prosaic cages.
Or are they in a tumbrel to a guillotine en route
to something less appealing than a lecture or a moot?

Are they *pagliacci* a kind of intellectual clown
dressed wigless in a suit and gold covered in a gown?
Or are they rustic yokels with charming village names
who've simply come to town to play some legal games?

Tango till you drop

A judicial tango show imagined in the Great Hall of the Royal Courts of Justice, Belfast

Abrazo clenched across the hall they in a frenzy go
milonguera close, small steps in syncopated show
and in the style of *pulpo* (that's octopus to you)
pasada here *arrastre* there and all in high heeled shoe.

Canyengue in one axis closed, now legs are slightly bent
sacada steps to fill the partner's empty spaces lent.
Judges and their partners jump dance float and spring
Zeoli's fingers dance across the chords and string.

Guitar it fills the stale and tepid legalistic air.
Magician of the instrument, the master plays with flair
a doctor of the ears to those who listen to things sadder
those tales of prisoners in their cells or botched operated bladder.

No more a cattle yard, a market stall, that marbled hall
aficionados through its portals the Tango Club now calls.
So come you all to Tangoland to the Camicando fest
By Zeoli's magic skill and by music be impressed.

Let's watch amazed gymnastic lifts and kicks and drops
till *boleos* and *ganchos* cease and till the music stops.

Abrazo -embrace milonguera – a social tango dance; pasada – step over; arrastre -drag step; canyengue- close embrace; sacada- displacing the other partner's leg; boleo- a backward and forward throw; gancho: leg hook

The Procession

The beginning of the Legal Year

A hush in sombre hall and then they come,
a wondering crowd and wives struck dumb,
horse haired accoutred   spaniel eared
these men who like to think they're feared
red robed like priests or martyrs dead
these men who think they call forth dread
strut out across the marbled catwalk tall
careful on their feet   can't afford to fall
sudden cross the floor and through the doors
expect to hear loud acclamations   roars
they sit in splendour on their chairs
their faces worn and tense with cares
in vain they listen for some rousing cheers
but hear the hum of snigger, unspoken jeers
(and sneers?)

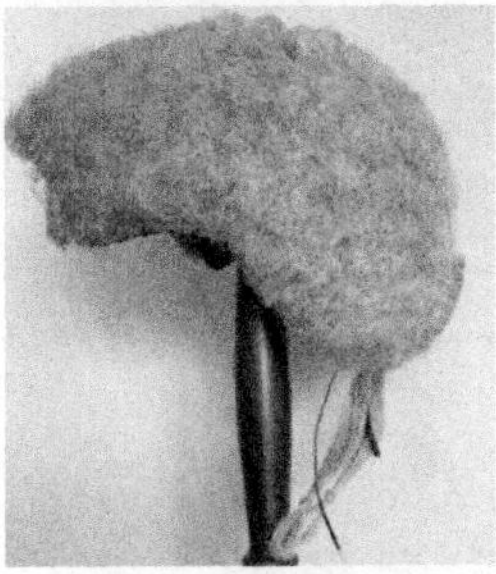

Day of Judgment

Black robed and wigged in fur enwrapped
in judgement seat he sits intense and rapt
and there before him tomes and papers sit
he fingers here a pleading   there a writ.

Affidavits wordy   bulging tedious long
Averments clearly true and others wrong
he listens to cascades of words and cataracts
which endless flow   disputed laws and facts.

Untruth's battalions float adrift on air
allegations here disputed versions there
somewhere firm ground must find to stand
amongst the moving tide and shifting sand.

How can he distil the core of truth from lies?
Onward he must trudge and inward sighs
but while true answer's really hard to say
he must resolve it all by judgement day.

A Sense of Tragedy

A Mirror Cracked

Reflections on the Ukraine War

Abounds not ugliness   black face of death
hard fists cold knives backstabbing joy by stealth.
The killing sprees of guns and children killed
the falling missiles raining unto graveyards filled.

The copious tears of widows tell out the cost
while golden crops in bomb filled fields are lost.
And yet abounds not beauty fair and true
the face of gentle love   and mercy too.

Close linked extending inter-touching hands
and eyes that see man's needs not warring lands.
A mirror twisted cracked reflects   distorts
bright colours dim   true beauty's lines contorts.

How ends the battle 'tween these rival twins?
Red heart of hate or love's embrace? Which wins?

The Trench

Picardy 1915

A gash slashed on fields' brown face
flows out from birches tall white barked
that sentient stand pale ghostlike sentinels
which watch the flows of mud and blood
rivulets that ooze and suck-slurping slop
feel winds and rains as bullets drop
smell acrid acid gas-filled drifting smoke
touch summer dust the clouds of drying clay
see uncut hay that turns to yellow grey
dry season's scabby crusted open wound
that once again in autumn's dripping days
bursts open raw anew to suppurate afresh
and freeze to shards in winter's cutting ice
cavern of unwashed stoics' unsaid fears
who stand in Hades' pools of unshed tears.

Picardy 1965

We laugh and grin young fresh we come
blue sky above a beaming smiling sun
a picnic day a day to play a day for fun
and out along the woodland path we tread
touch white crinkled papery birch tree barks
watch flittering fluttering busy nesting birds
we come upon a beckoning narrow open trench
that onward distant flows all soft green grassed
and down in we climb a velvet tunnel half
a primrose bower long dappled shadows dance
through tousled yellow broom that sun it glints
no cutting shards of winter ice no blood no mud
no rivulets of ooze no slurping clinging glar
wound cleaned and healed only now a gentle scar
the victor's laurel wreath on kind nature's head.

Darkness at Noon

The Jewish Museum Berlin

Hell is empty and all the devils are here
The Tempest (1,2) Shakespeare

There is a crack in everything and it is here the light gets in.
Leonard Cohen

Wie ein Tobender,wenn er in vollster
Raserei ins Schwarze stampft
Jählings am benehmender Gepolster.
Einer Zelle aufhört und verdampft

Like an insane man stumbling
headlong into the black
who ends up against the walls
of a padded cell and is vaporized

Rilke "Schwarze Katze"

Along museum corridors twisted intimidating
a door ominous. Open it go through
a void bottomless bleak black envelops
silence a shudder of emptiness cold chill.
stand motionless and disoriented. Be still.
Dead dread drips claggy clings and seeps
a blinding absence of light darkness at noon
and there above a tiny circle of light white
against an unremitting umbra obsidian.
Here is ghoulish metaphor spine chilling simile
in this black hole we stand in Auschwitz styx
in mind's eye and in the ear we see feel hear
anguish searing of those burnt who disappeared
endless up through a chink a chimney's mouth.
Where now the souls of those where did they go?
Innocents destroyed in Man's darkest night
Gone into everlasting shade or refound the light?

Designed by Daniel Libeskind the Libeskind Building in Jewish Museum in Berlin was opened in 2001. It contains amongst other exhibits the Holocaust Tower. The interior is black though a tiny amount of light falls from a higher opening. This poem reflects the intentionally profoundly disorientating and unsettling effect the exhibit has on those who stand within it and begin to sense the true extent of immeasurable evil of the Shoah.

Doolough

Some miles north of Delphi Lodge, a boutique country house hotel and former hunting lodge of the Earls of Sligo, lies Lough Doo near Louisburgh in Co Mayo. It is a place of sombre beauty and tranquillity with a somewhat foreboding atmosphere. Overlooking the lake is a memorial which marks one of the many human tragedies which occurred in Ireland in the middle years of the nineteenth century, the years of the Famine, what in Irish was called the Gorta Mór, the Great Hunger and the Drochshaol, the Bad Life. On 30 March 1849 two officials of the Westport Poor Law Union arrived in Louisburgh to ensure that people in receipt of outdoor relief were entitled to continue to receive it. The inspection was postponed and the two officials repaired to Delphi Lodge for dinner and to find a bed in what was no doubt a comfortable household. The people who had been told to gather for inspection were told to appear at the Lodge at 7 am the next day if they wished to continue to receive relief. For much of the night and day hundreds of destitute and starving people had to undertake a fatiguing journey in bad weather to arrive at Delphi. On the way many died including children. The local paper reported the deaths of at least 16 but local folklore speaks of

hundreds dying. Whatever the true figure it was a tragic and horrible event. This event exemplifies many of the features of the Famine, a seminal event in Irish history - human loss, death in horrible circumstances, the sundering of families, the destruction of the of the lives of children, unsympathetic bureaucracy, lack of human empathy and understanding, condescension to the poor and the weak, heartlessness in the face of an unfolding human disaster and a determination to maintain wealth, status and privilege. A cross and an annual Famine Walk between Louisburgh and Doolough commemorate the event.

Irish Proverbs

Is náire an saibhreas agus daibhreas ag an gheata
Wealth is a shame while poverty is at the gate

Ní thuigeann sách seang
The well fed do not understand the hungry

The rich man in his castle and the poor man at his gate

1840

Drizzle damp and grey long evening looms
glowers over moor sponged brown in gloom
o'er walls of stones clay sods all cold and wet
from rushy roof untrimmed rain drips like sweat.
No cottage this, unkempt a cabin rough makeshift
through broken door turf burning clouds adrift
weak heat weak light and round a weakling fire
unshod children clad in rags all torn and tired.
Across the growing dark bright eyed they stare
a family round potato pot communion share.
No cosy gospel manger no straw filled stable here
no angels and no lowing cows just want and hungry fear
the sounds of snuffle snorting of a pig that snaps
at fallen pratie skins and dirty measly scraps
that guest who helps to meet the endless need
to pay the rent to feed another's needs   and greed.

Granite fine a Georgian house well-built imposing site
o'er door the candles twinkle bright highlit fan light
within the sound of children playing aloud around
a playroom full of dolls toy soldiers laughing sound
within the clattering kitchen mouth-watering smells
the tinkling sound of calls to servants on the bells
that hang upon the wall transmit imperious command
of master or of mistress with this or that demand.
Comes carriage horse that stops beneath a porte cochère
arrived the evening's guests descending steps with care
protected from the damp from cold and pouring showers
the vestibule sweet smelling its vases full of flowers
warm welcome to a drawing room lit by roaring fire.
Well dressed and coiffed like English country squires
they sip their sherry wine from well-cut glistening glasses
condemn the feckless lazy the useless labouring classes.

1849

Across the moor a grey miasma mist it flows
through glassless windows drifting floats and goes
bearing the foul rancid stench of spuds that rot.
No trusty lumpers now to fill that family's pot
sore hunger etched round eyes no longer bright
no candles now or fire to even cast faint light
Deep darkness of the night reflected in the soul
of those who now must pains of famine thole.
How long have they before Grim Reaper comes?
How long before starvation pains grow numb?
How long before well-armed the constables evict
or other penalties impose or other pains inflict?
Chill sound of workhouse door hard slammed
within without on either side they're damned
or on a stinking ship out westward hopeful sail
and sink or swim and live to tell an awful tale.

Within the house still warm a turf fire burns
young master sits with governess and learns
reads stirring tales of Romans and of Greeks
knowledge of an ancient world and empire seeks
hears Bible tales of prophets miracles and love
is taught to bow his head before the God above
and still from out the kitchen rise smells of food
order reigns within that house and all is good.
For workhouse guardians great heaving table laid
glasses clink and pianoforte tunes are played.
Next day the chiming sound of seven on the clock
outside at door commotion noise and then a knock
door opens wide and there they stand unfed
the remnants of a starving band, the walking dead.
How many now can try or want to count or tell
how many at Lough Doo there froze and died and fell?

Sieh ich bin einer der alles	*Look I am one everyone has*
verlassen hast.	*abandoned*
Keiner weiss in der Stadt von mir	*no-one knows of me in this city*
Aussatz hat mich befallen.	*leprosy has befallen me*

Rilke

The Maharaja's Palace

Beside the marble gates red turbaned there they stand
exotic handsome guards who man an entrance grand
which opens to a court a yard all sparkling bright
where gleaming jewels glint on dazzling walls of white.

The firing raging zenith of a burning Indian sun
reflects a blinding light on silver urns that stun
which carried once to London the Ganges water gift
impassive there they stand impossible to shift.

.

Once washed an Indian prince in foreign heathen land
in empire's stately home afar from cows and sand
silver enough indeed the ills of life to cure
treasure enough to feed rose tinted Jaipur's poor.

Tasselled rugs heaped careless on unforgiving ground
soft footing for those guards to deaden passing sound
good beds for all those poor who endlessly endure
the unswept teeming streets in sleepless pink Jaipur.

Unlimbed at raja's gate poor lepers stand in row
to tourists passing through bow deep and very low.
The tourists stare at guards the shining walls the sky
look away on anything   to avoid sad lepers' eye.

The Valley of the Fallen
Valle de los Caidos

Silence and then a Goya scream
suppressed   flows out
from a jaw in a mountain cut
that gapes Hispanic hungry
a crocodile shedding false tears
slash-hacked hard unforgiving rock
raw knuckle blooded hammered
to the shouted screams of martinets
driving onward caudillo's prisoners
to build pomposity for a monster
a petrine offering to small man's ego
who bludgeoned new age heretics.
Polished marble granite a false skin
to cover over raw barbarous wounds
to entomb the skulls of dead underlings
driven on to untold untellable horrors
by old Spain its bloodlusts and sand

dying on the windswept burning hills
wounded like bulls taunted in a corrida
spirits hang-haunt in unforgiving gloom
in the belly of a hill   not of a whale
ghouls float in the chill of dark Hades
beckoning ghosts of the past   inquisitors
Torquemada hooded flagellants pyre makers
dark Felipe's doomed soldiers on Armada's tombs
conquistadors slashing their silver swords
dark souled Jew-baiting friars swinging beads
auto da fes entertaining mad kings and queens
burnt heretics   offerings to a strange deity.
Emerge from that ghost train unsettled
into the air and see that unremitting sun
that beat on fields of bloody hate and death.

Autos da fes; mass burning of heretics

The Valley of the Fallen outside Madrid contains a basilica built into the side of a mountain topped by an enormous cross. Constructed on the orders of General Franco the Caudillo supposedly as a memorial to the fallen in the Spanish Civil War it was in fact a memorial to the dead on Franco's nationalist side in that terrible conflict which cost the lives of hundreds of thousands and saw the commission of dreadful atrocities on both sides. Franco was buried there after his death but subsequently his remains have been removed. The Valley of the Fallen remains a deeply contentious site in the new democratic Spain.

A Sense of Occasion

The poet's eyes in a fine frenzy rolling.

\- *Shakespeare*

Poetry touches you at the melting point below the breast-bone and the beginning of the solar plexus

\- *Seamus Heaney*

I like the company of poets. They take us away from the boring reality of life

\- *Charles Haughey*

Visit to the Áras

On the occasion of a dinner hosted by President McAleese for the Judges of the Higher Courts in Ireland and Northern Ireland

Pearl chokered elegant erect she stands an t-Uachtarán
Black Beauty on her steps   Ardoyne's Maud Gonne
Mac Giolla Íosa's Máire gentler modern Markievicz
brings to the Áras Martin glamour and some glitz
like to a Yeatsian gazelle from Sligo's Lissadell
there in the presidential palace in Fionn Uisce's dell.

She greets the moving ranks of judges and their wives
flying columned men who judge men's lies and lives
turf smoked they move across the swirling Celtic rugs
acknowledged nods and glances kisses and some hugs
and keep the chitter chattering talking going
champagne and orange juice and Guinness flowing.

Then out across the flower lined pathway under tents
heat smoke and light from out the brazier vents
past floodlit play of water blue beside the lawn
into new Tara's hall of Cáit Ní hUallachán
amid the vast and eerie canvas painted fables
we all sit round the orange pumpkin laden tables.

October festive faces smiling bright and candle lit
we finish with a lemon posset and little dainty biscuit
as poet's moving eyes fine frenzied roll
observing things enriching soul and sometimes droll
connexions everywhere perceived   poetic nexus
enough to melt great Heaney's solar plexus.

Then comes a Middle European music treat a feat
a group of Slovak buskers from down Grafton Street
to finish off a night of friendship fun and craic
then out along the tented gravel path and back
back to the House to tea and coffee rugby scrum
a class of port a brandy digestif or rum.

Long fond farewells dictated by the tyrant time on clock
led back to bed by L C J the leader of our flock
and on the morrow shopping brunching lunching
Euros, switch and credit cards all crunching
A panic as we wait for missing judging lad
forgot the time (or was he mugged by someone bad?)

And as we sit all counted organised and bussed
he carefree comes   no hint of being non plussed.
Return we must to Haughian boredom of real life
back to those rows and endless litigation strife.

Putti in Farmleigh

On the occasion of a North/South JudicialColloque during the Financial Crisis in Farmleigh a former Guinness mansion in Phoenix Park Dublin now used as an Irish state guest house.

Floating on a boudoir wall grey painted *angeli*
the three dimensioned product of a Michael (Irish) Angelo
woven hangings on the walls silk plucked and wool
that graced the home of Guinness prince   no fool
black porter foaming once and still with cash
that fed a stream of opulence   an antiques' stash.

Greek gods aloft cast down their beady ancient eye
on Erin's brehons munching minted lamb who spy
and watch indebted nation drown its sadness
they banished for the night all talk of bankers' badness
they quick avert their gaze from debtors' chairs
and turn their table talk to gentler kind affairs.

They harken to the honeyed words of Irish saint
protector of the works of those who write and paint
to every cow its calf to every book its copy
and talk of music on the Internet hard drive or floppy.
The attic jury on the walls its mind and ears agog
awaits the brehons' clever words to dissipate their fog.

Next day the brehons' *mná* hear gaol doors heavy clank
and see the cells of Easter martyrs stale and dank
they turn awhile to see Narcissus' special place
Marsh's house of books but see no pool reflected face.
All over in a flash the end of Dublin days away
Go back again to work and still the putti play.

Putti – in art winged infants who either play the role of angels or act as instruments of profane love
Brehons - Irish judges
mná -wives/women

A Marriage made in Heaven

No more the parish spinster but now a radiant bride
looking simply stunning, Prince Charming by her side.
No more she turns the handle to spin her golden thread
a married woman now, helpmate spouse instead.

To home she rushes early to stoke the family fire
lay out her husband's slippers, with lipstick him inspire,
and fondly making tea she'll stroke his weary brow
delight in all his wisdom, an attentive listener now.

If out he stays quite late or overnights elsewhere
she'll brush it to one side, stay home and wash her hair.
To keep her beauty lasting she'll titivate her face,
for she's married now and settled, she surely knows her place.

Put Tanfastic on her cheeks and, yes, a bit of rouge
put water in the freezer and set up a vodka louge.

And married men have duties to do the things they can
it's a frightful heavy burden being a truly modern man
a culinary expert and considerate lover boy
a dad who goes to Mothercare and buys a cuddly toy.

Must rush into the kitchen to make a meaty pie
of Guinness, steak and gravy, perhaps of chicken thigh
then early go to bed, kiss his bride before he sleeps
then early rise from bed to go and tend the sheep.

Across the field he'll run and looking deftly slick
He'll learn the proper way to tackle and to kick.
Buy her bunches of cut flowers and jelly baby sweets
shop early for her prezzies and lots of Christmas treats.

Be truly a Prince Charming   no unpoetic toad
he must learn to pen some verses   romance her with an ode.

A Sense of Romance

Les Amants

Saint Valentine's Day

Are we lovers still awhile let's quiet ask
why should we hide the longings of our heart
wear upon our downcast face Venetian mask
and keep our once entangled limbs apart?

Lie not here like water bottles on our bed
to feel the dissipating heat grow sadly cold
wishing now a gentle touch and heated kiss instead
seeking the tenderness of old to catch and hold.

Let not bored Eros turn away his face and walk away
leaving, where once he was, a merely passing shade.
Let not the beauty of our passion have its day
or let the charms of love decide to go and fade.

Can yet awhile the ecstasy of love still flame
carry us still to pinnacles of height and light
and take us to that realm without a name
lifting and moving us in never ending flight?

If turning now and flying away let us call back
the wispy Cupid drifting off in trails of sighs
coax him gently to return along his beaten track
before he goes a sun eclipsed in darkened skies.

Within the temples of our body let us transcend
upward climb on Jacob's ladder earthly and divine
upon the wings of angels borne take flight ascend
give fully of ourselves and make thee surely mine.

A Sense of an Ending

The cycle of life

Rumpled crumpled paper sticks are made
a nest for turf or wooden logs arrayed
then friction rubbed   in hand pink tip
erupts a passion bright flames let rip.

The cackling laugh of growing flames alight
all juvenile at first   that playful sprite
the hearth an incandescent maturation
sparking scintillation scorched conflagration.

The orange flares of heat with violet fringed
by passing burning tongues the logs are singed
inbreathing suction of a chimney swept
up danced the fire and pranced and leapt.

Excitement built exuberance that soared
then slow decline and timber logs no more
wood blackened then to ashen cinders burned
from life to death and all to dust is turned.

Those embers spent   all heat turns cold
now dead that fire -   life story told.

Le Cycle de la Vie

Des papiers froissés chiffonnés qu'on construit
À recevoir les bûches comme un véritable nid
Embrassé par les flammes toutes passionnées
Allumées par une pointe rose très bien frottée.

Écoute le rire saccadé des flammes qui dansent
Comme des fées ludiques toutes pleines d'élégance
Vois une scintillation d'étincelles iridescentes
Un foyer vivace avec une vie incandescente.

Les bûches par des langues brûlantes flambées
Des flammes vacillantes couleur orange violet
Un feu qui danse   qui fringue   qui saute
Avalé   aspiré   par une cheminée haute.

L'excitation monte - quelle vie exubérante!
Déclinent alors les bûches fumantes
Le bois noirci tombe aux cendres brûlées
Et tout est mort tout écoulé tout écoulé.

Adieu cher ami   quelle vie transitoire.
Feu le feu   - la fin de sa brève histoire.

Muckish Co Donegal

Old Rosapenna Hotel

Long journey at an end and now a scrunch
car stops and parks on white pebbles yielding
to rubber tyres and sandaled children's feet.
Up wooden steps we rush veranda cross
into a palace of varnished wood brown built
the scent of burning turf adrift through doors
glass paned to a room where clattering cups
tinkle syncopate and voices quiet hum.

Upstairs we go deep within a displaced chalet
not snowy set but in the fabric of spun tweed
Donegal its washed greys and blues sand dunes
Muckish a water colour smudging scumbled clouds

hill-top mists bleeding into darkening purple hills.
Along corridors   each with its bucket of water
a bucket of sand   mere nods and a wink to a fire
that could consume a magician's jewel box.

Cases unpacked and down to lobster lunch we go
black tied and tailed the waiters seamless move
trundle trolleys loaded with temptation's treats
desserts and cheese those savouries and sweets.
Along the sandy path we go   past croquet lawn
past silent dunes that smothered once a village whole
Sheephaven Bay its changing colours, waves and winds
along a beach deserted empty foreboding at its end.

Where once that timbered palace stood all gone
a space wilded where once there was a verdant lawn
sedges brown tipped and prickled shrubs have taken hold
of dissipated dreams that billowed smokes enfold
no more the sounds of tennis balls on courts of tended grass
the click of croquet balls   the clinks of glass
the sounds of children's laughing play on seaside rocks

Consumed by flames that place of dreams   sad tinderbox.

Footnote

Rosapenna Hotel was built in 1893 by the Earl of Leitrim to attract golfers to Donegal. An unusual structure designed in Stockholm and built of wood it became a prestigious hotel famous for its cuisine and hospitality. Sadly, the old wooden structure burnt down in 1962. A newly constructed Rosapenna was built some distance away overlooking Downings Bay. The site of the old hotel is now overtaken by nature leaving little trace of what had been a unique and magical place.

Last line

Evening falling   the long day is done
a day for John of neither joy nor fun
the pain of broken lives spelt out
weighing up so many words and doubts
those affidavit lines that endless flow
that into scabby cicatrices grow
exhibits wrongly numbered careless tagged
wordy counsel he'd see gagged
and now he muses with a glass of gin
sets ice cubes and the lemon in a spin.

Come see says Jill   but John stays shtum
sour-faced and grim and melancholic glum
Just leave me be I have no wish to stare
I've had enough today   too many woes and care
of fighting brats   of battered wives and thugs
of drunken men fired up on drugs.

Oh! Do come John   this you must not miss
Jill only heard a sigh and then a hiss
gin drunk at last John stirs and up he rises
has no hope of seeing some kind surprises
too late he comes to see the golden setting sun
the rosy violet hues that would a mortal stun
dark light descending now and evening gloom
and quiet dimness fills the mood filled room
Just as I thought   there's nothing there
John turned round and slumped back in his chair.

Jill longed for tenderness of patient minds
at each slow dusk a drawing down of blinds.

This poem was written as a response to a challenge from my judicial colleague Sir Michael Nicolson thrown out to his judicial colleagues to to write a poem ending in the last line "And each slow dusk a drawing down of blinds." This is in fact the last line of Wilfred Owen's Anthem for Doomed Youth:

The pallor of girls' brows shall be their pall,
their flowers the tenderness of patient minds,
and each slow dusk a drawing down of blinds.

About the Author

As a senior barrister and then as a judge of the High Court and then of the Court of Appeal I wrote extensively on legal matters during a long career and now enjoy the freedom of creative writing particularly poetry which is often inspired by his travels, by nature, by his sense of place, history and time and by his career in law. A keen amateur artist my work is influenced by an eye for colour, form and atmosphere. I contributed a prose piece *Affairs of the Heart* to *The Heart of the Matter* (Imspired Press 2022) and poems to Issue 21 of the online magazine and the printed version thereof published by Impspired Press 2023. I was a contributor to North Coast Writers' 2023 Anthology *Spun Yarns and Woven Words.*

Acknowledgments

After I retired, I joined the North Coast Writers Group a Causeway Coast u3a group whose facilitator was the very talented and enthusiastic Mary Farrell. All the members of the Group owe her an enormous debt of gratitude for her stimulating leadership and for the amount of time and energy she has devoted to encouraging members of the Group in their creative writing. As a testament to her remarkable leadership capabilities several members of the Group have now produced their own publications of works. As I said in the Introduction Mary has encouraged me to add this collection of poems to the burgeoning North Coast Writers' library though I do so with some trepidation remembering the words of Thomas Kinsella *Ireland has many poets and most of them are no good.*

I am also most grateful to all the members of the Writers Group who are incredibly mutually supportive and encouraging. Their contributions and critiques of each other's work are always though provoking, inspiring and of the highest quality. Some of the poems are the result of writing stimulus exercises which the Group carry out in the course of their meetings.

I am particularly grateful to Sue Steging for her kind comments in the Foreword. She is a poet and writer the quality of whose own work has been justly recognised in the Seamus Heaney Award for New Writing in 2023. I am also grateful to Sir Reg Weir a fellow barrister and judge with whom I worked over many years and who encouraged me in the days of my judicial poetic forays. His wit and insights often inspired the Muse.

I thank all my former judicial friends and colleagues whose conversations and lunch time camaraderie stimulated not a few lines of poetry over the years some to be foun in the poems in this collecion

Causeway u3a has been very supportive of the activities of our writing group and I thank all the members of the Committee and members of an organisation which stimulates so many activities and enriches the lives of its members in so many different ways.

I thank my wife Karen for her support and encouragement and for the time she took to proof reading the work.

Poetry does not emerge in a vacuum and I pay tribute to all the people and places who have influenced my mind consciously and unconsciously. I shall never quite know from where all the ideas and thoughts that end up in a poem come. Perhaps most of all I must thank the Muse for her unpredictable visits and inspirations.

Literary acknowledgments

The poems *Florentine Dawn, In the Garden of Good and Evil, Samarkand, In Drumnamh Wood 1* and *Farewell to Turf* appeared in *Spun Yards and Woven Words* (published by Impspired Press 2023.) The poems *Kings College Chapel* and *La Salute* appeared in Impspired Press's online Magazine Issue 21 and the printed version thereof in 2023.

Printed in Great Britain
by Amazon

38304638R00076